D1315170

Black Duck and Water Rat

Introduction

Black Duck and Water Rat *is a story from the Dreamtime. This legend explains the origins of the curious platypus which first appeared many years ago in Australia. When Water Rat abducted Black Duck, and forced her to marry him, the result of their union was two strange little creatures who shared the traits of both parents. Their progeny were furry mammals which lay eggs, sport a leathery bill, and crawl along on four big webbed feet.*

The myths of the Aboriginal people spring from a time long ago when human beings were the only living creatures on Earth. The first human beings, who came from the stars, possessed supernatural powers. These ancestral beings brought the world into existence, creating the land and the sea. They brought knowledge, morality, and law. Life on Earth was good in that ancient time until cataclysmic changes rocked the land. Disaster came to Earth in the form of floods, volcanoes, droughts, and earthquakes. Fear moved many of the first ancestors to seek refuge in a most remarkable way. They transformed themselves into animals, birds, plants, insects — and even rocks — as they attempted to hide and protect themselves. It was during this tumultuous time of transition that Dreamtime commenced and the Earth came to be populated with the multitude of life forms we know today.

Author Percy Trezise grew up in the Australian bush which fostered his love of nature. In 1960 he met the aspiring Aboriginal artist, Dick Roughsey, whose Aboriginal name was Goobalathaldin. Together they began a partnership in painting, writing, and exploring, which endured 25 years until Roughsey's death. Trezise continues to document the legends and lore of the Aboriginal people through his painting and writing in this work with Mary Haginikitas. In 1983 he received the Advance Australia award for his outstanding contributions to Australian art and culture.

Library of Congress Cataloging-in-Publication Data

Trezise, Percy and Haginikitas, Mary.
  Black duck and water rat.

  (Stories of the dreamtime — tales of the aboriginal people)
  Summary: The kidnapping of a young female black duck by Goomai the
water rat gives rise to the platypus tribe.
  [1. Australian aborigines—Legends. 2. Platypus—Folklore] I. Trezise, Percy, ill.
II. Haginikitas, Mary, ill. III. Title. IV. Series: Stories of
the dreamtime.
PZ8.1.T72B1 1988   398.2'454'0994   [E]   88-20121
ISBN 1-55532-945-4 (lib. bdg.)

North American edition first published in 1988 by

Gareth Stevens, Inc.
7317 West Green Tree Road
Milwaukee, WI 53223 USA

First published in Australia by William Collins Pty. Ltd.

Editor: Kathy Keller
Introduction: Kathy Keller
Map: Mario Macari
Design: Kate Kriege

1 2 3 4 5 6 7 8 9 92 91 90 89 88

Black Duck and Water Rat

story and art by
PERCY TREZISE & MARY HAGINIKITAS

Gareth Stevens Publishing
Milwaukee

Long ago in Dreamtime, the young Mara lived with her people
beside a lily lagoon. Her people were called the Black Duck tribe.
Many other water bird tribes shared the lush flood plains.

4

Each dawn and dusk the plains were filled with a great noise. It was the voices of water birds announcing to each other where to find the best food.

5

They also told each other the hiding places of their enemies — the big snakes, the eagles, and Bunyip the water monster, who all loved to eat delicious water birds.

6

That very morning Bunyip had risen stealthily out of the water and gobbled down two members of the Black Duck tribe.

Time passed and Mara grew to be quite beautiful. Springtime
brought rain and rising waters. With friends, Mara visited other
lagoons and streams to feast on new, tender plants.

In her excitement Mara forgot her tribe's safety warning: always stay with others. She wandered off alone to nibble on sweet grass shoots at the water's edge.

Suddenly a huge water rat rushed from his hiding place and grabbed Mara. She struggled in terror, but the rat only laughed and held her more tightly.

He dragged her off to his burrow in the creek bank and said, "I am Goomai. You shall marry me and live with me. If you try to escape I will kill you."

Goomai slept during the day and hunted at night. On dark nights he sometimes let Mara out for a swim, but guarded her closely. How she missed the sun's warmth and light!

Mara pretended that she was happy to be Goomai's wife, and
Goomai began to believe that she was contented. One day, when
he was asleep, Mara saw her chance to escape.

Mara sneaked past sleeping Goomai and slipped silently into the
water. She swam away as fast as she could, watching over her
shoulder for Goomai.

She was still looking back when there was a great swirl of water.
Bunyip rose drooling from the deep, right in front of Mara.

Bunyip roared and lunged for her, but Mara hurled herself into the air. She felt his hot breath on her tail as she escaped the swish of his bony claws.

16

Soon she was far away from Bunyip and Goomai. Far above the
broad plains, she could see the lagoon of her people in the
distance.

The Black Ducks were astonished when Mara returned for they
thought she was dead. When she told of her life as Goomai's wife,
her mother held Mara and wept.

Mara loved being free. She splashed and played in the water all day and flew about with her friends at night. How good her life was once more.

When water filled the flood plains, the Black Ducks laid their eggs.
Some nested in hollow trees. Others made scrapes in the ground
among the grasses.

Mara laid her eggs in a tree stump's hollow shelter. She wondered
why her friends had eight or more eggs while she had only two.

21

When the ducklings hatched, their mothers soon taught them to swim. But Mara hid her babies, Baarli and Gayadari, because they were different. They were new creatures, called platypuses, part duck, part water rat.

At last Mara took her children to the water. Horrified, the Black Ducks hissed at Mara when they saw her platypus babies. They had fur, not feathers, and *four* webbed feet! "Leave or we'll kill them," they squawked.

But Mara loved her children in spite of their unusual appearance. She had to move, but where? Downstream lived evil Goomai and Bunyip. Here on the plains her own people had banished her.

24

She looked far away to the mountains that stood where the sun rose. The children squeaked with delight and played in the mud as they journeyed along the road to safety.

Finally they reached a sheltered pool high in the rain forest. The children burrowed through the side of the pool's bank to make their new home.

Baarli and Gayadari loved to dive and sift the mud for food. Often they sunned themselves on the rocks and combed the water from their fur.

Before long Mara's children were grown with families of their own. She had not seen them for a long time. The platypus babies swam away when they saw her.

One moonlit night as the wind sighed, Mara felt lonely. She longed for her own Black Duck people and she missed the lily lagoon. It was time for her to go home.

Baarli and Gayadari lived on happily in their rain forest home.
Soon they had many grandchildren who moved to other mountain
streams and pools.

There they all lived, a tribe apart, and it seemed to them it was always so. But in the camps of the Black Duck tribe the story of Mara and Goomai and the first platypus babies lives on.

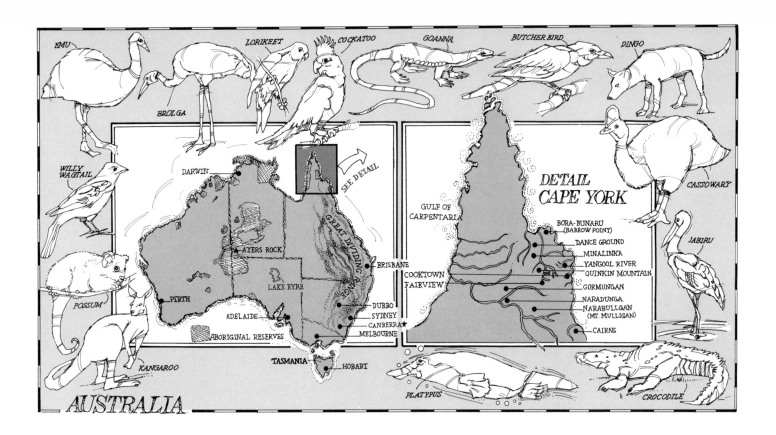

AUSTRALIA

DETAIL CAPE YORK

Glossary

astonished: filled with surprise or wonder
Baarli (BAR lee): one of the platypus babies in this story
Bunyip (BUN yip): the water monster in this story
Dreamtime: the time long ago in Aboriginal mythology when supernatural ancestors created the world
flood plains: a level region of land which is often covered with water from a nearby river during a flood
Gayadari (guy a DAR ee): one of the platypus babies in this story
Goomai (goo MY): the water rat in this story
lagoon: a shallow body of water separated from the sea by a coral reef or shoal
lunged: moved forward suddenly
Mara (MAH rah): the black duck in this story
platypus: a rare Australian mammal
rain forest: a tropical forest with at least 100 inches (254 cm) of rainfall each year
scrapes: shallow marks carved in the ground by water ducks forming the foundation of their nests
stealthily: with secret movements

CR
j new